PENPALS *for*
Handwriting

Year 5 Practice Book (9–10 years)

T0139684

By **Gill Budgell & Kate Ruttle**

Supported by the
National Handwriting Association
Promoting good practice

Contents

CAMBRIDGE
UNIVERSITY PRESS

Practise the letters. Now write each letter with
a slope that is comfortable and speedy for you.

l i t u j y

r b n h m k p

c a d o s g q e f

v w x z

Write your name in sloped writing.

Read and write
the words.

slope

slope

alphabet

alphabet

angle

angle

Speeding up
Rewrite at least three times
at an increasing speed:

*We use a slope
to increase
fluency and speed.*

Check:
- the slope of your handwriting.

Find two letters to tick and two to improve.
Rewrite them.

Practise the joins. Now write each join with a slope that is comfortable and speedy for you.

th   sh   nb   nd   ht   st

th   sh   nb   nd   ht   st

Write the rhyme to practise your slope.

Whether the weather be cold
Or whether the weather be hot,
We'll weather the weather
Whatever the weather,
Whether we like it or not.

Anonymous

Practise the pattern.

Read and write the words.

storm

storm

lightning

lightning

sunshine

sunshine

Check:
- the slope of your handwriting
- the joins to ascenders.

Find two words to tick and two to improve.
Rewrite them.

Practise the joins. Now write each join with a slope that is comfortable and speedy for you.

ai   ay   kn   er   ie   en

ai   ay   kn   er   ie   en

Write the text to practise your slope.

Do you know "The Rime of the Ancient Mariner", by Samuel Taylor Coleridge?

Research the poem and write out some of it for practice.

Practise the pattern.

Check:
- the slope of your handwriting
- the joins to letters with no ascenders.

Find two words to tick and two to improve.
Rewrite them.

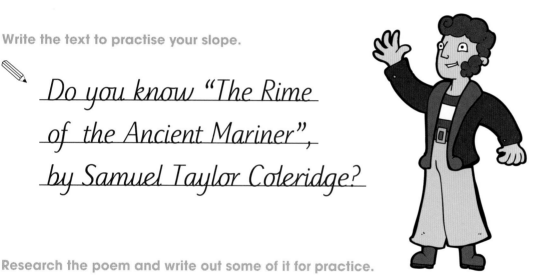

Read and write the words.

poem

poem

recite

recite

rhyme

rhyme

Practise the joins. Now write each join with a slope that is comfortable and speedy for you.

ac   sc   bo   da   ea   ho

ac   sc   bo   da   ea   ho

Join each of Set 1 letters to at least two of the Set 2 letters.

Set 1	Set 2	Example
a b c d e	*a c d*	*aa ad ba bc*
h i k l m	*g o q*	
n p q s t u	*s*	

How many combinations can you make?

Practise the pattern.

Check:
- the slope of your handwriting
- the diagonal join.

Find two words to tick and two to improve.
Rewrite them.

Read and write the words.

patterns

patterns

vowels

vowels

combinations

combinations

Practise the joins. Now write each join with a slope that is comfortable and speedy for you.

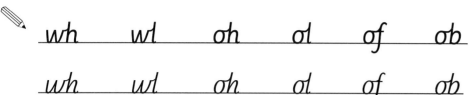

Write a question web. You might not use your best handwriting for this web, but make sure your writing is legible.

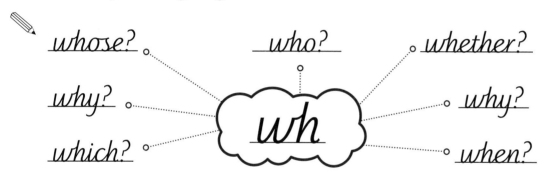

Choose a topic. Write it in the centre. Write a question about your topic using each word.

Practise the pattern.

Check:
- the slope of your handwriting
- the joins to ascenders.

Find two words to tick and two to improve.
Rewrite them.

6

observe

observe

symbol

symbol

knowledge

knowledge

Practise the joins. Now write each join with a slope that is comfortable and speedy for you.

oi   oy   ou   op   ve

oi   oy   ou   op   ve

Write the text.

I have found an old joke:
Which type of pop group did
The Young Mummies join?
A boy bandage!

Write your own joke.

Speeding up
Rewrite at least three times at an increasing speed:

That joke is
not funny.

Check:
- the slope of your handwriting
- the horizontal joins.
Find two words to tick and two to improve.
Rewrite them.

Read and write the words.

have

have

love

love

found

found

7

Practise the joins. Now write each join with a slope that is comfortable and speedy for you.

oo   *oa*   *wa*   *wo*   *va*   *vo*

oo   *oa*   *wa*   *wo*   *va*   *vo*

Join each of Set 1 letters to at least two of Set 2 letters.

Set 1	Set 2	Example
ow	*a c d*	*oa oc od*
r v	*g o q*	
f	*s*	

How many combinations can you make?

Speeding up
Rewrite at least three times
at an increasing speed:

*Keep letters clear
when writing
at speed.*

Check:
- the slope of your handwriting
- the horizontal joins.
Find two joins to tick and two to improve.
Rewrite them.

**Read and write
the words.**

footprints

footprints

wandering

wandering

vagabond

vagabond

Practise the joins. Now write each join with a slope that is comfortable and speedy for you.

ra   re   ri   ro   ru

ra   re   ri   ro   ru

Write the word list in joined, sloped writing. Keep the vowels in a line.

m a rvellous
diff e rent
descr i be
contr o versy
br u ise

Use a quick, but legible, handwriting to plan your own word list like this, showing the vowels in a line.

Practise the pattern.

Check:
- the slope of your joins
- your joins from *r*.

Find two words to tick and two to improve.
Rewrite them.

Read and write the words.

random

require

ridiculous

round

ruin

very

Practise the joins. Now write each join with a slope that is comfortable and speedy for you.

 sh   su   sc   sl   sw   sp

sh   su   sc   sl   sw   sp

Write the sentence in joined, sloped writing.

 She stared at her shiny shuffling shoes and screamed.

Write at least three scary sentences using these words.
Use a sloped, fluent handwriting style.

 shiver   soldier   shriek   snake
slither   astronaut   slide   skeleton
scratch   ghost   scar   stare

Speeding up
Rewrite at least three times
at an increasing speed:

Keep letters the correct size when speeding up.

Add prefixes or suffixes to change
the words if you need to.

Check:
- the slope of your joins
- your joins from *s*.
Find two words to tick and two to improve.
Rewrite them.

Read and write
the words.

strange

island

invisible

suspicious

fantasy

science fiction

Write the text out neatly but speedily. Use a slope that is comfortable for you.

The pterygotus, which was also known as the 'water scorpion', was one of the first land creatures. It lived about 300 million years ago and it could be up to 2 metres long.

Write a new heading for this text in your own handwriting style.

Speeding up
Rewrite at least three times at an increasing speed:

Keep the correct letter and word spacing when speeding up.

Write one benefit of sloped writing.
Write one disadvantage of it.
Write a handwriting target for yourself.

Read and write the words.

history

pre-historic

vertebrate

geology

museums

researchers

Practise the joins.

fl   fl   ft   ft

Write the text.

Tiger and Fire

In the beginning of the world, it was Tiger who owned the fire of the world. The fire flared as the flames flickered and flashed like fireflies. He fed it often so that the gift of fire flourished.

Speeding up
Rewrite at least three times at an increasing speed:

Keep letters in the correct letter proportions when speeding up.

Check:
- the slope of the join to ascenders
- the height of the *f* in relation to the *l* and *t*.

Find two words to tick and two to improve.
Rewrite them.

Read and write the words.

fable

soften

forest

thereafter

swiftness

inflection

Practise the joins.

fa   fe   fi   fo   fu

Write the heading. Write the text.

Fish fact file

* *fish have different numbers and kinds of fins*
* *freshwater fish may live in fast-moving rivers*
* *saltwater fish may live on coral reefs*

Speeding up
Rewrite at least three times at an increasing speed:

Regular letter sizing makes writing easier to read.

Check:
- the comparative size of all the *f* joins you have written
- your slope.

Find two words to tick and two to improve.
Rewrite them.

Read and write the words.

five

fifteen

fifty

fantastic

information

future

Write a paragraph about these facts.

Bat facts

- warm blooded

- only mammals able to fly

- babies called 'pups'

- have fur

- have thumb and 4 very long fingers

- many kinds; about 1,000 species

- feed at night

- hang upside down sleeping in
   a 'roost' in the day

Read and write
the words.

dashes

commas

brackets

clause

paragraph

parenthesis

Practise the pattern.

Check:
- the spacing of your letters and words
- your slope.
Find two words to tick and two to improve.
Rewrite them.

Practise the joins.

ff   ff   ff   ff   ff   ff

Write these words in alphabetical order.

baffled   *ruffled*

scuffle   *scruffy*

sniffled   *snuffled*

snuffle   *truffle*

Read and write the words.

duffle

handcuff

official

difficult

different

sufficient

Speeding up
Rewrite at least three times at an increasing speed:

The scruffy thing
snuffled and
scuffled away.

Check:
- the ascenders of ff are the same height, and the descenders are equal *ff*
- the slope.

Find two words to tick and two to improve.
Rewrite them.

15

Practise the join.

rr   rr   rr   rr   rr

Write out the speech bubbles.

I'm arranging the carrots.

Make way for my wheelbarrow.

Tasty berries and fresh cherries!

purr, purr

Hurry! Hurry!

Add another speech bubble featuring *rr* words.

Speeding up
Rewrite at least three times at an increasing speed:

Harry left in a hurry with a flurry.

Check:
- the joined *rr*s are the same size
- the layout of your writing
- legibility.

Find two words to tick and two to improve.
Rewrite them.

Read and write the words.

flurry

borrow

narrow

horrible

barrier

irregular

Practise the join.

ss   ss   ss   ss   ss   ss

Write out the poster.

Class Chess Club

We have assorted boards to choose from.
Impressive players.
Discuss key moves and assist others.

no experience
necessary

success is
possible

Practise the pattern.

Check:
- the joined *ss* are the same size and
  height as each other
- your slope.

Find two words to tick and two to improve.
Rewrite them.

Read and write
the words.

message

process

session

assistance

classic

successful

Practise the joins.

qu   qu   qu   qu   qu

Write the following paragraph using words from the box below.

Many _____ occur near the _____.
Earthquake response teams _____
specialist training and _____. They are
highly _____ and they must follow a
strict _____ of events in their responses.

> *equator   equipment   qualified*
> *require   earthquakes   sequence*

Speeding up
Rewrite at least three times at an increasing speed:

Queue quietly
with questions.

Check:
- the spacing between the *q* and the *u*
- your slope.

Find two words to tick and two to improve.
Rewrite them.

quest

unique

enquire

liquid

aqua

frequently

Try creating your own capital letter fonts that you might use on posters or invitations.

Here are some ideas to inspire you. Try each and then create some of your own.

Read and write the words.

QRST   UVWX   YZ   You choose!

font

text

letter

height

width

spacing

Speeding up
Rewrite at least three times
at an increasing speed:

*Choose the right
handwriting style
for the purpose.*

Check:
- sizing, spacing and proportion of each
  set of letters is consistent.
Find two letters to tick and two to improve.
Rewrite them.

Write the months of the year in sloped, joined writing. Then write them in upright print writing.

Read and write the words.

January   *January*   *July*

February   *August*

March   *September*

April   *October*

May   *November*

June   *December*

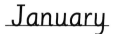

month

calendar

weekly

planner

diary

electronic

Speeding up
Rewrite at least three times at an increasing speed:

different styles of handwriting for different purposes

Check:
- your slope
- your print letters
- your capitals.

Find two words to tick and two to improve.
Rewrite them.

Write the text. Answer each question with true or false.

The fact is that information technology is very exciting, but digital devices and games require us to follow precise instructions in a sequence if we are to be effective.

Write out the statements that are true.

1. I can write notes in scruffy handwriting if it is legible.
2. The best handwriting for a sign or label is joined and sloped.
3. Print alphabet has no exit flicks and letters are upright.
4. Sloped writing should be leaning backwards.
5. A slope may be less useful for left-handed writers.
6. Uneven spacing of letters or words is tricky to read.
7. It doesn't matter if two letters bump together.
8. Short ascenders make letters confusing e.g. is it n or h?
9. Long descenders can get mixed up with the letters on the line above.

Give yourself a mark out of **10** for the neatness of your handwriting.

/10

Work with a partner to check you have identified the rules that are true.

Read and write the words.

systems

programs

input

algorithms

networks

output

Practise the joins.

ph　　ph　　pl　　pl　　bl　　bl

Write and continue the short story. Focus on parallel, sloped, downward strokes.

The pharaoh put a blanket on the elephant's back and rode triumphantly to the peoples' applause. They blew whistles and cheered to show their complete pleasure in his courage. The elephant, although a simple beast…

Continue using as many *ph*, *pl* and *bl* words as you can.

Speeding up
Rewrite at least three times at an increasing speed:

The pharaoh put a blanket on the elephant's back.

Check:
- your slope
- the parallel lines of *p, b, h, l.*

Find two words to tick and two to improve.
Rewrite them.

Read and write the words.

complete

complain

plough

autobiography

physical

valuable

Practise the joins.

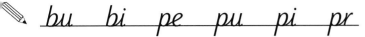

bu   bi   pe   pu   pi   pr

Write a list of each animal and its preferred food type.

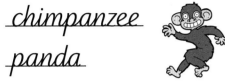

chimpanzee
panda
hippopotamus
polar bears
leopard
baboon

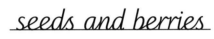

bamboo
impala
seals
seeds and berries
bananas
grass plants

What sort of handwriting did you use for this list?

Speeding up
Rewrite at least three times at an increasing speed:

Quick but legible writing is fine for notes and lists.

Check:
- that your list is neatly set out
- that your list is legible
- your joins from *p* and *b*
- you included a break at *z* in chimpanzee.

Find two words to tick and two to improve.
Rewrite them.

Read and write the words.

parakeet

especially

panther

humpback whale

punctuation

binoculars

Practise the joins.

bb   bb   bb   pp   pp   pp

Write the words. Add, remove or replace prefixes to make words with the opposite meaning.

bb or *pp* word	Opposite
unabbreviated	_____
disapply	_____
appropriate	_____
approve	_____
reappear	_____
appealing	_____

Speeding up
Rewrite at least three times at an increasing speed:

It disappeared, then reappeared with a wobble, and we clapped.

Add at least two more *bb, pp* words to the list.

Check:
- how parallel your ascenders and descenders are for *p* and *b*
- your slope.

Find two words to tick and two to improve. Rewrite them.

Read and write the words.

equipped

wobble

clapped

approve

rubbish

supplementary

24

Practise the joins.

bb   cc   ff   gg   ll   mm
oo   pp   rr   ss   tt   zz

Write the words with their missing double letters.
Use all of the above examples at least once.

1. co____led
2. a____o____odate
3. a____re____ive
4. a____ached
5. marve____ous
6. su____icient
7. mu____le
8. emba____a____ed
9. o____ortunity
10. stu____orn
11. ba____n
12. whi____ed

Read and write the words.

agree

harass

communicate

accompany

possession

dissatisfied

Speeding up
Rewrite at least three times
at an increasing speed:

Marvellous, whizzy
communication.

Check:
- size
- spacing
- proportion.
Find two words to tick and two to improve.
Rewrite them.

Practise the joins.

tial   tial   cial   cial

Write this text at speed. Time it.

This is an official TV commercial.
Torrential rain is initially expected
on Monday and there is potential for snow.
Take special care when travelling.

Now assess it and try again to improve your handwriting and speed.

Practise the pattern.

Check:
- your slope
- the joins *tial* and *cial*
- capital letters
- legibility of your writing at speed.

Find two words to tick and two to improve.
Rewrite them.

Read and write
the words.

social

especially

essential

partial

crucial

spatial

Practise the joins.

ie   ei   ie   ei   ie

es   ies   ves

Write each word in its plural form. Write quickly and smoothly.

vein   *variety*

belief   *dictionary*

loaf   *ceiling*

butterfly   *protein*

thief   *niece*

Now assess your writing and try again to improve your fluency.
Make your writing flow.

Practise the pattern.

Check:
- your slope
- the joins
- the loops of your *e* in *ie* or *ei*
- the legibility of your writing.

Find two words to tick and two to improve.
Rewrite them.

Read and write
the words.

sieve

veil

field

series

friends

kaleidoscope

Write this text in your own personal style. Write neatly and fluently.

Friends

I have a friend who likes knotting and
one who likes knitting. I know others
who enjoy climbing and boxing, and one
who just knuckles down to hard work.
But me? I like no hustle and bustle; it's
thumbs up to an island life for me.

Practise the pattern.

Read and write
the words.

castle

column

library

wrinkle

Autumn

asthma

Check:
- your personal style.
  How would you describe it?
- the joins
- the neatness of your writing at speed.

Find two words to tick and two to improve.
Rewrite them.

Practise the print alphabet.

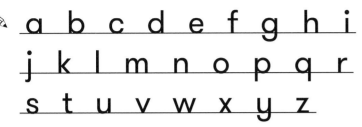

a b c d e f g h i
j k l m n o p q r
s t u v w x y z

Print these words to label the diagram of the eye. Write a caption in print letters.

pupil
eyelid
tear duct
iris
eyelash

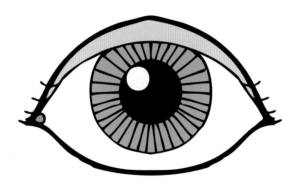

Speeding up
Rewrite at least three times at an increasing speed:

different
handwriting for
different purposes

Check:
- your print letters
- spacing.
Find two words to tick and two to improve.
Rewrite them.

Read and write the words.

label

diagram

clarity

printing

form filling

address

Write the jokes and answers in a joined, sloped handwriting style that is comfortable for you.
Then use the questions opposite to self-assess your handwriting.

Q. What reads and lives in an apple?
A. A bookworm.

Q. What's worse than finding a maggot in
your appple?
A. Finding half a maggot in your apple.

Write this word family. Add to it if you can.

joke   limerick   pun   riddle
homophone   homonym

Find your own maggot or worm joke to write out.

Use these questions to assess your own handwriting. Give yourself a mark out of 12.

1. Is your writing mostly joined when it should be?

2. Is the slope of your writing always the same?

3. Have you used print script correctly?

4. Are your descenders and ascenders parallel?

5. Are your descenders and ascenders clearly different from your x-height letters?

6. Is the spacing between letters and words even?

7. Are your x-height letters the same size?

8. Are your capital letters the same size?

9. Have you laid out the jokes neatly?

10. Did your hand move smoothly over the page as you wrote?

11. What are you most pleased with?

12. What do you need to improve?

Score   /12

Write the rules for capital letters.

CAPITAL LETTERS

1. NEVER JOIN CAPITAL LETTERS.
2. MAKE THEM THE SAME HEIGHT
   AS ASCENDERS.
3. ALWAYS BEGIN AT THE TOP.
4. USE THEM TO BEGIN SENTENCES.
5. USE THEM FOR PERSONAL
   NAMES AND TITLES.
6. USE THEM FOR EMPHASIS.

Read and write
the words.

RULES

POSTERS

PERSONAL NOUNS

EMPHASIS

CLARITY

VOLUME

Practise the pattern.

Check:
- capital letter formations for *E M K Y N*.
Find two words to tick and two to improve.
Rewrite them.